Ms Caterpillar's 'The Dazzling Mango'

Concept, Written & Illustrated by Arti Bal

Also in the series:-

Ms Caterpillar's 'The Apple'

Ms Caterpillar's 'The Banana'

BLUEROSE PUBLISHERS
India | U.K.

Copyright © Arti Bal 2023

All rights reserved by author. No part of this publication may be reproduced, stored in a retrieval system or transmitted in any form or by any means, electronic, mechanical, photocopying, recording or otherwise, without the prior permission of the author. Although every precaution has been taken to verify the accuracy of the information contained herein, the publisher assume no responsibility for any errors or omissions. No liability is assumed for damages that may result from the use of information contained within.

BlueRose Publishers takes no responsibility for any damages, losses, or liabilities that may arise from the use or misuse of the information, products, or services provided in this publication.

For permissions requests or inquiries regarding this publication,
please contact:

BLUEROSE PUBLISHERS
www.BlueRoseONE.com
info@bluerosepublishers.com
+91 8882 898 898
+4407342408967

ISBN: 978-93-6452-039-3

First Edition: October 2024

To all those who look forward
to the season of Mangoes
and to Mitto, our darling Parrot
who filled our lives with
Love and joy.

Hello!

My name is Ms. Caterpillar..

I am going to give you lots of information about one of my favourite fruits..

'The Mango'

India is the largest mango producing country in the world. There are over 1000 varieties of mangoes cultivated in India.

DID YOU KNOW?

- **Mango** trees need lots of sunlight, humidity and rich soil.
- A **Mango** tree bears fruit within a period of 4 to 8 years after planting.
- **Mangoes** ripen in the summer season and are ready to eat.
- **Mango** trees have been growing in India for the past 5000 years.
- Every part of a **Mango** tree is used for various medicinal purposes.

Uttar Pradesh is the largest Mango producing state in India. Some of the varieties cultivated here are Chausa, Dasheri, Langra, Mallika, Amrapali, Fazli, Gulab Khas.

There are amazing stories behind every variety of Mango. The names given to the Mangoes are related in some way to the history behind their birth. One such story is of Langra/Langda.

It is believed that in 1800s a fakir/hermit in Varanasi, planted a mango seed in his backyard. A tree grew from the seed which bore delicious fruits.

The fakir was crippled and people, crudely, called him 'Langda'. It means cripple in Hindi. The Mango was named after the fakir as 'Langda Aam'.

STORY

This is my imaginary story of the Langda Mango from Uttar Pradesh.

Once there was a Mango sweet and delicious. Although he was delicate and small, he had way bigger dreams. You see, he had an adventurous streak in him. He wanted to jump and fly from every branch. And so he did. But he had to pay a price.

The little Mango fell and broke his legs everytime he jumped. But he never gave up. Everytime he fell, his drive to fly got bigger.

He believed that we all fall but it is about learning to pick ourselves up. This Mango tried harder and harder. All those injuries made him limp but it did not break his will.

He found ways to continue fulfilling his dreams. It gave him the freedom and happiness that was beyond compare. His legs were broken and so, he was named *'Langda'. But his mind and spirit were unbreakable.

*Langda - In Hindi language, langda means 'One who is crippled'

Some popular varieties of Mangoes cultivated in India

Alphonso — 10–12 cm

Alphonso, the King of Mangoes, also known as Hapus is cultivated mostly in the Konkan region of Western India. It has a very deliciously rich, creamy and non-fibrous pulp.

Kesar — 10–12 cm

Kesar, the queen of Mangoes, has a very delicious bright orange coloured pulp and is grown mostly in the Indian state of Gujarat.

Langda — 8–10 cm

Langda or Banarasi Langra is grown in many North Indian states. A fully ripened Langra Mango has a greenish skin and a sweet pulp.

Chausa — 13–15 cm

This aromatic and sweet flavoured Mango has a high nutritional value and is mostly grown in Bihar and Uttar Pradesh.

Banganapalli — 12-15 cm

This delicious Mango has a thin, smooth skin with yellow firm non-fibrous pulp. It is mostly cultivated in the Indian state of Andhra Pradesh.

Imam Pasand — 10-12 cm

Also known as Hamam Mango, it has a soft skin and a unique taste. It is grown mostly in Southern states of India. It was once considered the Mango choice of the rich and the royals.

Rumani — 6-8 cm

This South Indian variety of Mango is also known as the Icecream Mango or the Apple Mango because of its delicious flavour and its small size.

Malgova — 10-12 cm

This fairly large Mango is sweet, juicy and fragrant. It is mostly grown in the Southern states of India.

Dasheri — 9-15cm
This sweet and aromatic variety of Mango is one of the most beloved. Originally cultivated in Uttar Pradesh, It is now grown through-out North India.

Neelum — 10-15cm
It is a delicious juicy and fragrant Mango with numerous health benefits. It is mostly grown in the south Indian states of Karnataka, Tamil Nadu and Andhra Pradesh.

Amrapali — 9-10cm
This hybrid Mango is a cross between Dasheri and Neelum. It was developed by Dr. Pijush Kanti Majumdar in 1971. It is now cultivated across India.

Mallika — 8-10cm
This hybrid Mango is a cross between Neelum and Dasheri. It has a non-fibrous delicious sweet pulp. It grows well in places with Tropical climate.

Fazli — 12-14 cm

This fairly large mango is primarily cultivated in the Indian state of West Bengal. It has a pleasant smell and is quite sweet and juicy.

Himsagar — 9-12 cm

This non-fibrous variety of mango is cultivated mostly in the Indian state of West Bengal. It has a sweet taste with slight tartness.

Chokanan — 15-20 cm

Originally from Thailand, this sweet mango is now grown in India. It is also known as Miracle mango because the tree bears fruits twice a year.

Bombay Green — 10-12 cm

Also known as Malda, this hybrid mango has a sweet taste and a non-fibrous orange colored pulp. It is cultivated mostly in North India.

Did you know?

Haji Kaleemullah Khan, famously known as 'Mango Man', is an Indian horticulturist and fruit breeder. Using grafting techniques, he was able to grow around 300 different varieties of Mangoes on a 120 years old Mango tree. He recieved the 'Padma Shri' Award for his extra ordinary contribution to Horticulture.

He continues to do many such experiments.

My memories of the orchard with
one Mango tree,
Laden with fruits hanging
till my knee;
Sounds of joy filling the air,
Friends and sisters laughing
without a care;

Plucking the unripe Mangoes,
breaking them against the trunks,
Fighting over the pieces,
to get the biggest chunks;

Mother opens the wrapped up paper
with salt and chilly,
Bingeing on the Mangoes
without feeling silly;
Licking our fingers till our
eyes and mouth feel sour,
Heart filled with exuberance,
that beautiful time was ours.

Fun Facts:-

Mango is one of the oldest fruits of the World. It appears in the historical evidences dating back to 25-30 million years ago in parts of India and South east Asia.

The cultivation of Mango started around 5000 years ago. In the 14th century, the Portugese traded for Mango seeds and fruits and took them to other parts of the World.

The Portugese called it Mango which comes from the Tamil word "Mangkai" and the Malayalam word "Manga" which means raw Mango.

Mango was originally also called "Amraphal".

Salsa!

Salsa is a latin dance originating from Cuba.. and also this famous dip.

Ingredients: Green Chillies, Mango, Onion, Tomato, Capsicum, Avocado, Pomegranate, Coriander or Mint leaves, Lime/Lemon, Salt, Pepper

Recipe :-

Combine all the chopped fruits and vegetables in a bowl. Add lime juice, salt and pepper. You can make your own recipe by adding or removing ingredients as per your taste. Enjoy salsa with home made chips and nachos. For healthier version, have salsa with toasted flat bread (rotis) or fresh crunchy iceberg lettuce.

Baked Mango Cheesecake!

Make no Mistake,
This recipe is not a Fake.
Bake this one for foodie's Sake
The epicure in you will Awake
Your taste buds will Shake
You will Escape,
To the Wonderland of Cake!

Ingredients

For the Crust:-
200 gms of Homemade Butter Cookies or store bought plain, ginger or coconut cookies.
- 3 tbsp melted butter.

For the Topping:-
200gms of mango curd Recipe in the Jams & Preserves section.

For the Filling:-
675gms or 3 cups of cream cheese
150-200gms of sugar depending on the sweetness of your mangoes
3 tablespoon of cornflour
2 cups of Mango Puree
1 tbsp lime juice
3 tablespoon butter
4 large eggs
a pinch of salt.

Method:-

1. Put the cookies in a zip lock bag and bash them into a coarse powder.

2. Add melted butter and mix nicely.

3. Pour the mixture in a 9 inch baking dish (lined with butter paper).

4. Pat down the mixture with a spoon and refrigerate for atleast 10 minutes.

5. Whisk the cream cheese into a smooth paste.

6. Add the powdered sugar and rest of the ingredients. Mix nicely.

7. Pour the batter in the prepared dish.

8. Bake at 150°C for 75-90 minutes.

9. Once done let it cool completely then spread the mango curd and refrigerate for couple of hours to set. Decorate with mango pieces or seasonal berries. Slice and Enjoy!

No Bake Cheesecake!

No Eggs No Flour, It's still a cake;
Got zing got flavour, it's quite easy to make,
Put the ingredients together, No need to bake.

Ingredients

- Dish lined with cling film or baking paper.
- Homemade cottage cheese or Paneer - 1 cup or 200 gms
- Whipping cream - 200 ml.
- Powdered sugar - 2 tablespoon
- Mango pulp - 1 cup.
- Homemade butter cookies or butter cake - 1 cup coarsely ground.

Method:

- Blend the cheese into a smooth paste. Add the mango pulp and mix well.
- Whip the cream with powdered sugar till stiff peaks form. Add a few drops of lemon to speed up the process.
- Gently fold in the cheese mixture into the whipped cream.
- Pour the batter in the prepared dish and top it up with the cookie or cake crumbs and press down gently. Refrigerate overnight.
- Flip the cake carefully onto a plate. Decorate with mangoes and seasonal berries. **Enjoy!**

Mango Curd

Ingredients

With Egg
- Mango Puree - 200gms / 1½ cup
- Egg Yolks - 4
- Lime juice - 2 tbsp
- Sugar - 50gms
- Unsalted butter - 90gms
- Lime zest - 1 teaspoon

Without Egg
- Mango Puree - 200gms / 1½ cup
- Cornflour - 4 tablespoon
- Lime juice - 2 tablespoon
- Sugar - 1/4 cup / 50gms
- Unsalted butter - 6 tbsp
- Lime zest - 1 teaspoon

Here is the method:-

- Put all the ingredients (except butter & zest) in a saucepan. Mix well then keep the pan on a low flame. Keep whisking for 3-4 minutes till the sugar melts.
- Add room temperature cubed butter one by one. Whisk well after each addition.
- Continue whisking and cook for another 6-8 minutes.
- When the mixture starts coating the back of a spoon, it's done. Take it off the heat and stir in the lime zest.
- Store in airtight glass jars and refrigerate for couple of hours before use. **Enjoy!**

When you're in a Pickle,
Your heart feels Brickle,
World as cold as an Icicle,
Let the ache Trickle,
Don't let it Prickle,
Call a loved one, someone who can
Make you laugh, with a Tickle;
How they make your pain vanish with
just a hug, it's Magical.
That's how you know, they aren't Fickle,
Hold on to them, they are precious,
They aren't any dime or Nickle.

Mango Pickle

One of the methods to pickle Mangoes is by using vinegar and a variety of spices depending on your recipe. It is enjoyed as an accompaniment for adding flavour to numerous dishes.

Another method to increase the shelf life of Mangoes is by storing them in brine solution with some condiments. Pickling is to enjoy Mangoes during off-season and it has some health benefits as well.

Jam!

You can make it at home.
Yes Sir! Yes Ma'am!
This is no spam!
Just three ingredients,
A little of your time,
There you go, Bam!
You got your Jam!

Ingredients:-
- Mangoes → 4 cups of mangoes cut into small pieces
- Sugar → 1/2 - 1 cup depending on the sweetness of your mangoes.
- Lemon → 3-4 tablespoon lemon/lime juice

Method:-
Add the 3 ingredients in a saucepan and cook on a low-medium flame for about 30-45 minutes till it has a non-runny thick consistency. Let it cool then store in airtight jars & refrigerate.

Enjoy!

Enjoy with breads or buns or with your desserts!

Preserve:-
The only difference between jams and preserves is that you have to put larger chunks of Mangoes while making preserves.

COOL RECIPES

*It's summer time, you've got Mango,
You wanna chill, you wanna Tango
Let's make icecream, let's make sorbet
It's so much fun,
You'd make them everyday!*

Instant Mango Icecream

Ingredients:-
- 2 cups of frozen ripe Mango pieces.
- ½ cup of full fat cream or thick yogurt.
- 2 tablespoon honey if Mangoes are not sweet enough.

So easy to make:-

Put the frozen mango pieces, honey and half of the cream or yogurt in a blender. Blitz for a few seconds. Now add rest of the cream/yogurt and blitz again for 10-15 seconds till soft and creamy. Relish immediately!

Mango Icecream

Ingredients:-
- Fresh Mango Puree - 3 cups
- Condensed milk or sugar - 1/2 cup
- Whipping cream - 400ml or 2 cups

Method:-
- Put the cream and sugar/condensed milk in a bowl and whisk till stiff peaks form.
- Fold in the mango puree and freeze for couple of hours. Scoop and Enjoy!

Mango Sorbet

Sorbet is a frozen dessert made without any cream. Here is a simple recipe for you to try.

Ingredients:-
- Frozen Mango pieces - 2 cups
- Lime juice - 1 teaspoon
- Honey or Maple syrup - 1/4 cup

Method:-
- Put the frozen Mango pieces & lime juice in a blender.
- Blend for a few seconds then slowly add honey.
- Blitz again and store in the freezer for couple of hours. Scoop & Enjoy!

Shakes and Smoothies

Shakes are made by blending fruits or dry fruits with milk as the base.
Sugar is added for sweetness.
Natural or artificial flavourings can be added for taste.
Mango shakes are very popular during the Mango season.

Smoothies are drinks made purely by blending one variety of fruit or few different varieties of fruits.
A little water can be added to ease the blending.
No sugar or flavourings are added, making it a very healthy drink.
Smoothies are thicker in consistency than shakes.

Mango Juice

Ripe Mango Juice

Ingredients
- Ripe Mango puree → 2 cups
- Water → 4 cups
- Sugar → 1/4 cup
- Lime juice → 2-3 tsp

Method:
Just mix all the ingredients in a jug. Add some ice cubes and enjoy your refreshing summer drink.

Raw Mango Juice aka Aam Panna

is one of the most beloved summer time drinks in India. Here is a simple recipe to try.

Cook 2 large mangoes in water till they are tender. Take out only the flesh and blend it with 1/2 cup sugar, 8-10 mint leaves, 1/2 tsp each of pepper, roasted cumin powder and cardamom powder. Add 3/4 tsp of salt / black salt.

Take 2-3 tsp of the blended puree in a glass. Add water and ice cubes. Enjoy!

MANGO LOAF CAKE

Let us make a yummy Mango Cake,
Ask your loved ones to partake
Together its fun when eggs you break
Time spent with each other is Love, let's not fake.

Ingredients :-

- Flour - 2 cups
- Unsalted butter - ½ cup
- Sugar - 1 cup
- Eggs - 3 large or 4 small
- Mango Puree - ½ cup
- Baking powder - 1 tsp, Baking Soda - ½ tsp
- Vanilla essence - 1 tsp

Let us make the cake :—

- Beat the unsalted butter and sugar in a bowl till light and fluffy
- Add mango puree and vanilla essence or extract. Beat well.
- In a small bowl, whisk the eggs
- In a seperate bowl, sift the flour with baking powder and baking soda.
- Alternately add the whisked eggs and the sifted flour to the butter mixture, little by little. Pour the batter in a cake pan.
- Bake in a preheated oven at 180°C for 45-50 minutes. **Enjoy!**
- Substitute for Eggs :—
Take 2 tablespoons of flax seed powder and soak in about 8 tablespoons of water. Keep it aside while you prepare the rest of the ingredients. Add in place of the eggs in this recipe.

A hoopoe saw his friend Goose,
really sad, in the blues.
What happened asked the Hoopoe
to the Goose.
I want to woo my love, my forever Muse.
Should I schmooze her, with my coos,
How should I make her choose?
I am scared she will refuse.
Try something new, a different hue
Can you write Poems or Haikus?
Take her for a ride in the Canoe.
Get her some bright exotic blooms
She is different, sighed the Goose
Not easy to Amuse..
Does she have a sweet tooth?
Yes !! Said the Goose.
Then let's make her a yummy
creamy 'Mango Mousse'!!

Mango Mousse

Ingredients:-
- Whipping Cream or Coconut cream - 1 cup
- Sugar - 2 tablespoon
- Lime juice - 1/2 tsp
- Mango Puree - 1 cup
- Home made cake (flavour of your choice) or Home made biscuits (Ginger/coconut would be nice)

Easy Peasy Lemon Squeezy:-
- Whip the cream with lime juice and sugar till stiff peaks form.
- Gently fold in the Mango Puree.
- Crumble the cake or biscuits and make layers with the Mango mixture in a glass bowl or tumblers. Garnish with Mango pieces. Refrigerate to set. **Enjoy!!**

Mango Fruit Roll aka Aam Papad

Aam Papad is one of the most beloved snacks of India. It is available throughout the year to enjoy the flavour of Mangoes.

Two types of Mango Fruit Roll can be made. One with ripe Mangoes, which is mostly sweet. The other is made with raw mangoes and this is mostly sour with spices added to it.

The city of Amritsar, in the Indian State of Punjab, is famous for Aam Papad or Mango Fruit Roll.

Ingredients to make Aam Papad:—

With Ripe Mangoes
- Ripe Mango Puree - 1 cup
- Sugar - 2 tablespoon
- Cardamom Powder - 1/2 teaspoon

With Raw Mangoes
- Raw Mango Puree - 1 cup (Cook raw Mango till they are tender then Puree the flesh)
- Sugar - 1 tsp
- Powdered Spice Mix - 1/2 tsp each of cumin, red chilly, black salt.

Method:—

- Cook the Puree with sugar on medium flame. Stirring continuously till it thickens. Add the respective spices and cook for couple of more minutes.
- Apply ghee (clarified butter) to a stainless steel plate. Spread the mixture evenly in the plate. Cover it with a cotton cloth. Keep it in the Sun for atleast 2 days to dry. Cut it into strips. Enjoy!
- Alternatively, spread the cooked mixture in an oven proof dish lined with butter paper. Set the oven at the lowest temperature. Keep the dish in the oven for 3-4 hours to dry. Cut it into strips. **Enjoy!!**

Interesting Facts

🥭 Every part of a Mango tree, from roots to leaves; from bark to stem; from flowers to fruits, are beneficial to our health and our ecosystem.

🥭 Mango tree can grow well in dry and arid regions also. So, Mango tree farming can provide employment oppurtunities with good returns to the farmers.

🥭 Mango tree has extensive root system which prevents soil erosion. The organic matter like fruits and leaves fallen from the tree helps in soil conservation.

- 🥭 Flowers, leaves and fruits of Mango trees have numerous health benefits and are used in making traditional medicines for treating many diseases.

- 🥭 Mango Trees contribute to the biodiversity of our ecosystem by providing habitat for various animals, birds and other small creatures.

- 🥭 Mango Trees have the ability to reduce the Green House Effect, through photo-synthesis, by absorbing and storing large amounts of carbon-dioxide in their trunks, branches and leaves.

Story Time!

Once in a small forest with beautiful trees there lived many birds and animals. There was one huge and magnificent tree in the middle of the forest. It was a Mango Tree.

This mango tree bore the sweetest Mangoes in the entire region. Birds and animals from far away places came to eat Mangoes especially from this tree. The tree was laden with hundreds of Mangoes in the season.

In a nearby tree, two parrots made their home in a small hole. The mother parrot laid eggs in the nest. When the time came, the eggs hatched and little baby parrots were born.
One of the baby parrots was very inquisitive. Let us name her 'Paro.'

Paro went to the edge of the nest everyday and peeped out to see the big beautiful Mango tree. It used to wonder when her wings will be strong enough to fly to the Mango tree and eat one of those juicy Mangoes.

The day came very soon and she could fly to the Mango tree and eat the sweetest Mangoes as she had imagined. Since then she would relish the Mangoes every season.

One day Paro saw birds crying and panicking around the Mango tree. She came to know that humans were planning to build a road through the forest and hence many trees were being cut down.

The big Mango tree was going to be cut too. This made Paro very sad, but she was determined to do something about it. She sent a message to all the birds in and around the forest.

The day the tree cutters came to cut the Mango tree, all the birds from eagles, crows, parrots to tiny sparrows came and sat on the branches of the big Mango tree. They all started chirping and cheeping loudly.

When the tree cutters came close to the tree, the birds flew past them very closely. The men were taken aback, but still they moved ahead to cut the tree. Seeing this, the birds started attacking the men. Now the men really got scared and ran away.

When the road contractor was told about the situation, he came to visit the tree. He was a kind man. When he saw all the birds on the Mango tree, he understood their problem and made a decision.

After a few days, the road was constructed but it went around the big Mango tree and many other trees in the path.

A board was fixed near the big beautiful Mango tree. It read, "This Mango Tree belongs to the birds and animals of this forest. It is not to be touched". All the birds and animals enjoyed the delicious Mangoes from this tree for many seasons.

FUN FACTS

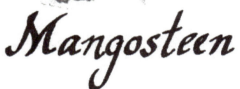
Mangosteen

Kokum

In India, Mango is the King of fruits and Mangosteen is the Queen of fruits. It is a juicy and fibrous fruit packed with flavours and health benefits.

Another variety of fruit in the Mangosteen family is Kokum. This fruit is famous for its juice and it is enjoyed as a cooling drink during summers.

The key to breathe free
is to go on a planting spree
Don't you all agree?
Let us each plant one
Mango Tree.

I hope you enjoyed my book on Mangoes.
I will see you soon with more on my
favourite fruits. Until then,
Eat your fruits,
Stay healthy,
Keep Smiling!

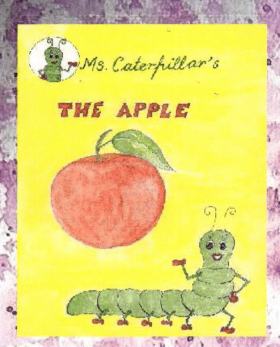
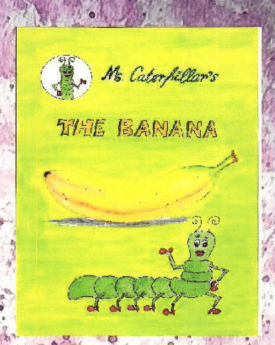

Ms Caterpillar's
The Apple

Ms Caterpillar's
The Banana

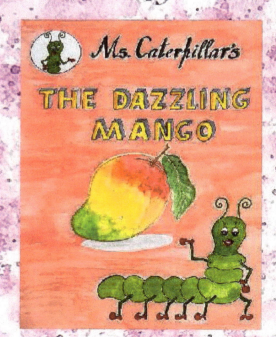

Ms Caterpillar's
The Dazzling Mango

Can you guess
the next ?

Milton Keynes UK
Ingram Content Group UK Ltd.
UKHW052224171124
451301UK00005B/78